"Those planning liturgies, whether for parishes or small groups, will find this a valuable help. In a form that is appealing and accessible, it opens up for the people the spirituality that flows from Christian use of the Psalms."

Dr. Bernard Cooke
Professor of Theology
Holy Cross College

"These translations of the psalms bring new and sometimes surprising thoughts to mind as Cleary puts them into modern language. They are good for us today since they help us see new meanings in them. I especially like his original psalms; they are prayers for people of our day.

"The book will serve a real need in providing brief, simple, and meaningful prayer services for parish meetings, and meetings of all sorts. The variety of themes is excellent."

Rev. Tom Kramer, Pastor
Cathedral of the Holy Spirit
Bismarck, N.D.

"In *Psalm Services* William Cleary gives us a creative celebration of prayer and poetry. He reaches beyond the poetic form of the psalms to their essence, the intensity of feeling beneath the surface structure. This is language charged with meaning. To meditate with this text is to journey through the range of human emotions and longings that bring us from festivity to silence, from darkness to peace.

"William Cleary makes the psalms accessible in all their wonder and poignancy, with all their strength and durability."

Dr. Anthony T. Padovano
Author, playwright, theologian, lecturer

PSALM SERVICES FOR PARISH MEETINGS

WILLIAM CLEARY

TWENTY-THIRD PUBLICATIONS
Mystic, Connecticut 06355

Illustrations by William Baker

Twenty-Third Publications
185 Willow Street
P.O. Box 180
Mystic, CT 06355
(203) 536-2611
800-321-0411

© Copyright 1992 William Cleary. All rights reserved. Permission to reproduce these psalm services—including the music—is granted only for the convenience of those who will use them in communal prayer services. They may not be reproduced for commercial purposes.

ISBN 0-89622-510-0
Library of Congress Catalog Card Number 91-68558

Dedication

Dedicated to Rahner's *Rudes*,
that circle of faithful rustics
with whom I have prayed
—and learned to pray—
for more than ten years,
with gratitude to the Holy Spirit
for always joining us.

Contents

Introduction	1
Psalms of GATHERING	
Blest Are They (Psalm 119)	4
You Are My Heart's Home (Psalm 16)	6
God of the Unexpected (Psalm of Tolerance)	8
Grant a Meeting of Minds (Psalm of Community)	10
Psalms of SEARCHING (Advent)	
In You I Trust (Psalm 25)	12
Come, O God, and Open Our Eyes (Psalm 85)	14
How Long Must We Wait? (Psalm of Endurance)	16
Psalms of DISCOVERY (Christmas)	
Sing a New Song (Psalm 98)	18
Forgive Us Our Debts (Psalm of Forgiveness)	20
Psalms of WORSHIP (Epiphany)	
All the Earth Is His Nation (Psalm 72)	22
Let All the World Sing (Psalm of Joy)	24
Look Into the Soul (Psalm in Silence)	26
Psalms of DARKNESS (Lent)	
Why Have You Forsaken Me? (Psalm 22)	28
Out of the Depths (Psalm 130)	30
Music: Taste and See	33
Taste and See (Psalm 34)	34
Messiah, Jesus, Yeshua, Christ (Psalm in Silence)	36
Psalms of LIGHT (Easter)	
This Is the Day (Psalm 118)	38
Give Thanks to God (Psalm 136)	40
My Heart's Applause (Psalm of Appreciation)	42

Psalms of PEACE & JUSTICE **(Pentecost)**
    Bless My Descendants (Psalm in Silence)   44
    Into Your Hands (Psalm 31)   46

Psalms of JOY & FAITH
    Send Forth Your Spirit (Psalm 104)   48
    In Memory of You (Psalm in Silence)   50

Psalms of MINISTRY
    My Light and My Hope (Psalm 27)   52
    If Today You Hear God's Voice (Psalm 95)   54
    Praise God for Our Enemies (Psalm of Trust)   56
    Make Us Disciples (Psalm of Devotion)   58

Psalms of LOVE FOR GOD
    Bless Your God (Psalm 103)   60
    Creation's Composer (Psalm of Confidence)   62

Psalms of RETREAT
    Come, Hear My Prayer (Psalm 17)   64
    My Soul Longs for You (Psalm 63)   66
    How We Do Blunder (Psalm of Honesty)   68

Psalms of CARING FOR EARTH
    I Will Praise Your Name Forever (Psalm 145)   70
    Music: God, O God of Wonders   73
    God, O God of Wonders (Psalm 8)   74

Psalms of SENDING FORTH
    Your Eyes Have Searched My Soul (Psalm 139)   76
    I Am Filled With Anxiety (Psalm in Silence)   78

Index   80

PSALM SERVICES FOR PARISH MEETINGS

Introduction

The 150 "Psalms of David"—composed by many hands over some 700 years—have been through the ages the favorite prayer book of many Christians. Their hardy directness and arresting imagery have been much loved, even though more than a hundred generations have passed since the psalmists wrote them. Meanwhile the faith that inspired them has traveled to every part of the globe. It is always a voice larger than life that speaks. And of course it is usually the *community* at prayer.

The psalms chosen here for these "gathering prayers" are some of those whose poetry and passion transcend time, and whose words can withstand a respectful updating, bringing them into the demanding semantic milieu of our own times, so justifiably concerned with inclusive and non-sexist language and conceptualization. Even before St. Jerome's "Christianized" translation of the psalms in the fourth century, the classical texts had been constantly "updated," since the most original texts are said to be often so obscure that no one can say *exactly* what the original meanings were. We paraphrase them, where necessary, with love and respect.

Jesus of Nazareth knew and quoted a number of the psalms. It is exciting to think that, through using the psalms ourselves, we can enter, however slightly, into those mysterious prayerful times of his, mentioned explicitly eleven times in the New Testament.

The psalms are not only a book of prayers but a textbook on prayer itself, teaching us how to make up our own prayers in a fashion both intimate, honest, and experiential. In this spirit I have added to this book of psalms some original psalm-like meditations, some for antiphonal reading, some for silent consideration.

HOW TO USE *PSALM SERVICES FOR PARISH MEETINGS*
Meetings are holy times, and wherever they are held is sacred space. That was Jesus' promise: "Wherever two or three are gathered in my name, there am I." "Sacred space" is not just space that seems sacred. God really is with us. So our rituals do not create artificial moments but rather bring us down to reality. But these rituals must be artful if they are not to seem artificial. Artful preparations for these holy times can make all the difference. The arrangement of chairs and tables, the position of candles and of symbols, the light and sounds in the meeting room: all these things make a difference.

Psalm Services for Parish Meetings can help provide the verbal element. Add to it human ingenuity of your own, your own plans for using what is presented here.

Reading over the service and the Gospel reading in advance are highly recommended. Decisions can be made at that time about variations you choose to include: a time for spontaneous prayers and the community response to these. ("Hear our prayer, O God" or "Blest be our God forever" work well.)

Most important: consider who the people are who are meeting, and what is their purpose, and what is the liturgical season. If all this can be ascertained in advance, the choice of an appropriate psalm service will be much easier. Be sure to use the cross-referenced indexes in the back of this book to select the psalm service for particular occasions or liturgical seasons.

Most of these services are designed for antiphonal reading (first one group or individual, then another reads). Designate your groups, if any, in advance so that the service can proceed without unnecessary interruption.

The "poetic psalms," those not from the scriptural book of psalms, may often best fit smaller, more intimate groups. The five "Psalms in Silence" are included for meetings where there is time and the desire for reflection.

Two pieces of music are included—with notes for the keyboard and chordings for the guitar—to spice up this spiritual cookbook. May the results be both tasty and wholesome.

William Cleary

TRUE BELIEVERS
Blest Are They
from Psalm 119

CALL TO WORSHIP
Leader   May the Spirit of God be with you.

All   And also with you.

Leader   We approach you, Creator of us all, not only as individuals today but as a group, a circle, a community of faith, a gathering of a part of the human family. We turn to you with one voice made up of our many voices, one heart made up of many hearts. You see us both as we are and as we desire to be. Grant us our desire to be together in prayer, and to reach to you in the darkness of mystery.

All   Blest be God forever.

ANTIPHONAL PSALM
*(Group A—or Leader—reads **bold** lines. The others read regular lines.)*

Blest are they whose way is blameless
   who walk in your light
Blest are they who know your guidance,
   who seek for you with all their heart

     Your strong voice guides our footsteps
       we stay securely on your paths
     Grant me skill to wait and listen
       so I will always hear your voice

Look kindly on your faithful servant
Keep me reverent of your words
Open up my eyes that I may appreciate
   the wonders of your way

     Come, teach me, God, your way of wisdom
       that I may know your voice
     Teach my heart to ever seek your way
       and follow it with all my strength

RELATED GOSPEL READING
Matthew 13:1-9, 18-23   Jesus tells the parable of the sower.

SILENT MEDITATION

Leader   For a few minutes in silence, let us pray to our God in secret.

CONCLUDING PRAYERS

Leader   "Lord, teach us to pray" is our own prayer today. Let us recite together the Lord's Prayer, imagining the infinite God as a dear and kindly father.

All   Our Father, who art in heaven, hallowed be thy name, etc.

Leader   Invisible Creating Spirit, you have gifted us with human understanding and intelligence so that we may find our way through the wonderful maze of creation that leads to you. We give thanks for the marvels around us and for the seeds of discovery that are sown in the fields of our lives. May we celebrate some day the rich harvest that grows from faith, and the joy of the final possession of life beyond death.

All   Blest be God forever.

REST IN GOD
You Are My Heart's Home
from Psalm 16

          CALL TO WORSHIP
Leader   May the peace and grace of our Gracious God be with you.

All   And also with you.

Leader   Spirit of God, give us the gift of prayer. We know not what to ask for when we pray, but we depend on your presence within us. Be with us in our words and in our thoughts, in our minds and in our hearts.

All   Amen.

ANTIPHONAL PSALM
*(Group A—or Leader—reads **bold** lines. The others read regular lines.)*

Preserve me, O God, for in you I take refuge
I say to my God, you are my heart's home
    I have no rest apart from you
    My God, my chosen portion and my cup
    Your love and care mean everything to me

In the night also my heart instructs me
and I find you, God, right there before my eyes
    Because you hold my hand, I shall not fear
    Therefore my heart is glad, and my soul rejoices
    My body also dwells safe and secure

For you point out to me the path of life
And in your presence there is a richness of joy
    Preserve me, O God, for in you I take refuge
    I say to my God, You are my heart's home

RELATED GOSPEL READING
Luke 22:52-53   Jesus is arrested.

SILENT MEDITATION

Leader   In silence let us entrust ourselves forever into the hands of God. *(After a period of silence, the leader goes on.)*

CONCLUDING PRAYERS

Leader   "Lord, teach us to pray," asked the apostles. Let us now pray the prayer Jesus taught them, picturing God as a good father.

All   Our Father, who art in heaven, hallowed be thy name, etc.

Leader   May the Spirit of God bless us all with a faith that is deep and lasting, and give us the enrichment of a community where the confidence and courage of others can inspire our own lives. Holy Presence within and around us, we are your children, full of weakness and ignorance now, but confident that our destiny lies with you, in the light of your face, and the comfort of your eternal life.

All   Amen.

OPENNESS TO ALL
God of the Unexpected
Psalm of Tolerance

CALL TO WORSHIP

Leader   May the grace and peace from God and Christ Jesus our Lord be with you.

All   And also with you.

Leader   Holy Spirit of God, so silent that we sometimes forget your presence, so invisible that we can imagine we are alone, open our ears and eyes to the evidence of your actions in our hearts and throughout the universe.

All   Amen.

ANTIPHONAL PSALM
(Group A—or Leader—reads bold lines. The others read regular lines.)

Dear God of the Unexpected, of the Unfamiliar, of the Unheard Of
   open my heart to the diverse human beings around me
   in all their unfamiliarity, differentness and surprises
      I may not be particularly good at bearing with diversity
      I am uneasy with certain people oftener than I'd like
      I'd like to take myself more lightly
         to learn now the openness I did not learn earlier in life
         to be more tolerant, not of evil, but of otherness

All innocent otherness is your very creation, Divine Spirit
   your will and design, your formula for this world
   of which I am a part, in all my own otherness
      I am no model of the way people should be
      My particular culture is no standard for everybody else
      My set of tastes, my ways of living and acting, are not a norm
         not for the whole world, the real world

This world is your circus... of the unexpected, the unfamiliar, the strange
   even the weird, the outlandish, and the baffling

What is it but snobbishness, arrogance and conceit
>that gives me the presumption
>>that everything should accommodate itself to me
>>should fit my tastes and preferences

Holy Source of All That Exists, nothing is more "other" than you!
>**nothing more full of the unexpected**
>**the unfamiliar, and the mysterious**

From many perspectives, O Living God,
>I am myself utterly different, strange, and inaccessible
>and I am able to judge rightly none of the people around me.

So, open my heart to all this multiplex human creation
>**help me to see myself as I am**
>>**just one living person among billions of the same**
>>**all different, and in many ways, all equal**

Give me the graciousness to say "yes" to what is
and "thanks" for the honor of being a part of your mysterious world

RELATED GOSPEL READING
Matthew 19:13-15 Jesus shows special care for children.

SILENT MEDITATION

Leader   For a few minutes of silence, let us appear before Christ as children, totally accepted by him with all our incompletenesses and imperfections. *(After a period of silence, the leader goes on.)*

CONCLUDING PRAYERS

Leader   Let us conclude with the Our Father, the prayer our Lord taught his disciples to pray.

All   Our Father, who art in heaven, hallowed be thy name, etc.

Leader   May the gracious inspirations of God fill us with courage and energy for a more acceptant and tolerant life, with openness especially to all the human race in every country and in every condition. Grant us, Holy Mystery, Creator of all that is, enough confidence in you and in your creation that we will have no lasting fear of the future, and no irreconcilable memories of the past.

All   Amen.

GRACE TO BEGIN
Grant a Meeting of Minds
Psalm of Community

CALL TO WORSHIP

Leader   May the Spirit of God be with you.

All   And also with you.

Leader   Grant us the grace, Holy God, at this moment—to pray: to pray as our own hearts are lifted up to you, to pray through your holy Word of psalm and Gospel, and to find words to speak in the silence of faith and trust.

All   Blest be God forever.

ANTIPHONAL PSALM
*(Group A—or Leader—reads **bold** lines. The others read regular lines.)*

Grant us, Guiding God, a meeting of minds
    a meeting of those baffling faculties we have to think with
    a meeting and an understanding of each other's thoughts and values
Grant this almost impossible request at least where it is crucial
    where injury or destruction will follow if we fail

    Dear God of Understanding
      You whose mind comprehends each least variation
      in all of creation's colossal variety
        You whose mind meets every other mind with perfection
        not missing a nuance or premise or illusion or conviction
        in all the uncountable minds of all time and in all space

Grant us, God of Understanding, some smallest share of your understanding
    at those times when we *must* understand

    For human minds seldom meet very well or for very long
      Each of us not only learns slowly, moment by moment
        but we find ourselves learning illusions, lies and errors
        just as fast as we learn the truth
      and often people grow apart if they do not listen to each other
        when it's important to have a harmony of minds

Give us, then, a meeting of minds
> **most of all with all those we love and want to love**
> **at least a *considerable* meeting, a good-enough understanding**
>> **so we can proceed from there even into the land of community**
>>> **where *many* minds attempt to meet**
>>>> **and understand what matters**

> Our world seems ever more like Babel
>> with everyone speaking a different language
>>> so that understanding—and community—becomes impossible
> Save us, your community, from that tower of despair

Give us such a level of respect for each other
> **that we will listen and listen again**
> **even when we've failed, even often, to achieve a meeting of minds**
> **for there is nothing more important for love**
>> **than a meeting of minds**
>> **to base love on**

RELATED GOSPEL READING
Matthew 5:38-48   Jesus tells the disciples to be merciful as God is merciful.

SILENT MEDITATION

Leader   For a few minutes in silence, ask for the gift of "a heart skilled in listening." *(After a period of silence, the leader goes on.)*

CONCLUDING PRAYERS

Leader   "Lord, teach us to pray," asked the disciples, and this is our prayer too. Let us now recite the prayer which the Lord Jesus taught to them, imagining the infinite God as a father.

All   Our Father, who art in heaven, hallowed be thy name, etc.

Leader   We give thanks, God of all creation, that we have the blessing of community and the advantages of knowing the Gospel, for in the wondrous light of your presence and grace, we can be confident that we shall have your guidance along our life's way, in the gracious company of our Lord, Jesus Christ, and of our fellow believers.

All   Blest be God forever.

GUIDANCE OF GOD
In You I Trust
from Psalm 25

CALL TO WORSHIP

Leader   Grace and peace to you from our Gracious God.

All   And also with you.

Leader   Dear God, who sows the seeds of promise everywhere despite the chilling presence of danger in the world, teach us to speak to you with confidence always, for we know you hear every prayer and answer it even before we utter the words.

All   Amen.

ANTIPHONAL PSALM
*(Group A—or Leader—reads **bold** lines. The others read regular lines.)*

To you, Holy Spirit, I lift up my soul
I wait for the advent of wisdom and justice
> To you, Holy Spirit, I lift up my soul
> I wait for the advent of wisdom and justice

My God, in you I trust
> **let me never be put to shame**
> **let not my enemies exult over me**
>> To you, Holy Spirit, I lift up my soul
>> I wait for the advent of wisdom and justice

Make me to know your ways, Holy One
> **teach me your paths**
Lead me in your truth, and teach me
> **for you are the God of my life**
>> To you, Holy Spirit, I lift up my soul
>> I wait for the advent of wisdom and justice

For you I wait all the day long
Be mindful of your mercy, O God
   and of your steadfast love
    for they have been my life from of old
      To you, Holy Spirit, I lift up my soul
      I wait for the advent of wisdom and justice

RELATED GOSPEL READING
Matthew 3:1-12 Matthew recounts the preaching of John the Baptist.

SILENT MEDITATION

Leader   Let us wait in silence for the voice of God, speaking in our inmost hearts. *(After a period of silence, the leader goes on.)*

CONCLUDING PRAYERS

Leader   "Lord, teach us to pray," asked the disciples. Let us now recite the prayer that our Lord Jesus taught them, imagining, for the moment, the infinite God as a father.

All   Our Father, who art in heaven, hallowed be thy name, etc.

Leader   We give thanks for the blessing of knowing you, gracious God, and of knowing your comforting presence. We rejoice to think we are in your heart, and that you look on us as would a perfect parent. We eagerly await the coming of your reign, Holy One, and we rejoice to know that you have it in your power to guide us in your ways, and to strengthen us for all that lies ahead in our lives.

All   Amen.

ADVENT
Come, O God, and Open Our Eyes
from Psalm 85

Leader   CALL TO WORSHIP
The grace of the Lord Jesus Christ, the love of God and the fellowship of the Holy Spirit be with you.

All   And also with you.

Leader   Fill us with hope, Holy God, for we live in a world full of despair and our own hearts are often heavy laden. As you were able to inspire so many faithful people over the ages, so fill us with that same enthusiasm and faith.

All   Amen.

ANTIPHONAL PSALM
*(Group A—or Leader—reads **bold** lines. The others read regular lines.)*

Come, O God, and open our eyes
so we may believe in your care

    Come, O God, and open our eyes
    so we may believe in your care

I hear God's voice from the highest hill
As the poor cry out for peace
Help is near when we turn to God
and worship and justice increase

    Come, O God, and open our eyes
    so we may believe in your care

Kindness and truth shall meet as friends
And justice and peace shall kiss
Truth shall spring from the fertile earth
and compassion fill every abyss

    Come, O God, and open our eyes
    so we may believe in your care

Look, God comes with a wealth of gifts
Our flowers shall turn to the light
Justice shall bloom where God has walked
and Mercy sprout up overnight
> Come, O God, and open our eyes
> so we may believe in your care

RELATED GOSPEL READING
John 21:25   John the Evangelist speaks of the many unknown works of Christ.

SILENT MEDITATION

Leader   Let us create in ourselves an inner psalm of silence and gratitude. *(After a period of silence, the leader goes on.)*

CONCLUDING PRAYERS

Leader   As Jesus taught his own disciples to pray, let us now address the Infinite God as a kindly father.

All   Our Father, who art in heaven, hallowed be thy name, etc.

Leader   Give us, Holy Spirit, an enlightened view of this mysterious world, and an awareness that your holy reign comes about in an infinite and uncountable number of ways. And may your blessing, Eternal God, the peace of Christ, and the fellowship of the Holy Spirit be ours, now and forever.

All   Amen. Alleluia.

WAITING FOR GOD
How Long Must We Wait?
Psalm of Endurance

CALL TO WORSHIP

Leader   May God grant you peace and grace.

All   And may the grace of God and the peace of Christ be with us all.

Leader   Holy Spirit of God, lead us into the mystery of waiting. We trust that you will be able to bring meaning out of all apparent chaos, and something of value out of all our pain.

All   Amen.

ANTIPHONAL PSALM
*(Group A—or Leader—reads **bold** lines. The others read regular lines.)*

Dear God, how long, how long must we wait
  before there will be an end to our agonies?
    You are our rock and our stronghold
    With you all things are possible

This burden is heavy labor indeed:
  just to wait
    in solidarity with all in the human family who wait
    with mothers waiting to give birth
    with children waiting to be fed
    with fathers waiting to be hired
    with parents waiting for lost children to be found
    You are our rock and our stronghold
    With you all things are possible

We can only pour our miseries into the chalice with theirs
  wordlessly joining in the pain and sorrow of all the world
    knowing only that at least we are not alone
      we have each other
      and we have you, Most Compassionate, Parenting God.
    You are our rock and our stronghold
    With you all things are possible

With your help, Gracious God, we can endure this together
   and even with some hope in our hearts
   for the clock is ticking and time is on our side
   and we have your promise
      that ultimately our hope is not in vain
      our faith is not in vain
   and our wordless solidarity is full of resurrection promise
      You are our rock and our stronghold
      With you all things are possible

For Jesus, our sacrament of solidarity, was your beloved child,
   He endured the role of suffering servant
   and lives now, with all our once-wounded race, in glory. Amen.

RELATED GOSPEL READING
Luke 22:19-20 Jesus offers himself in solidarity.

SILENT MEDITATION

Leader   Let us in silence "wait for God." *(After a period of silence, the leader goes on.)*

CONCLUDING PRAYERS

Leader   Teach us to pray as your son, our Lord, Jesus of Nazareth, taught his own disciples. We use his words.

All   Our Father, who art in heaven, hallowed be thy name, etc.

Leader   May the God in whom we have believed bless us with patience and love, and with the perseverance to wait until God's good time has arrived. Give us, Holy God, the grace you gave to Mary, the mother of the Messiah, as she waited to greet God's own son into the world. Together with Mary and all the saints we magnify God's glory and praise, now and forever.

All   Amen.

INSPIRED CHRISTMAS
Sing a New Song
from Psalm 98

	CALL TO WORSHIP
Leader	May the grace of our Lord Jesus Christ be with you all.
All	And also with you.
Leader	Holy Creator, we are filled with new light by the coming of our Messiah. May we so live in the light that we may be a source of illumination to those around us, and a joy to those we love.
All	Blest be God forever.

ANTIPHONAL PSALM
*(Group A—or Leader—reads **bold** lines. The others read regular lines.)*

Sing a new song in the House of God
   for the wonders of earth abound
The marvels of God's mysterious ways
   call forth a Day of Joy
      All the ends of the earth have seen
         the wonderful works of God.

Our God wins love and reverent praise
   from every part of the globe
God's fairness toward all the creatures on earth
   means justice will long be praised
      All the ends of the earth have seen
         the wonderful works of God.

All the ends of the earth have seen
   the wonderful works of our God
Sing joyfully, all you continents
   break into festive song
      All the ends of the earth have seen
         the wonderful works of God.

> **Take the harp to give praise to God**
>> **with songs of sweetest sound**
> **With trumpets and strings and drums and horns**
>> **sing joyfully unto our God**
>>> All the ends of the earth have seen
>>> the wonderful works of God.

RELATED GOSPEL READING
Luke 2:15-19 Shepherds visit Bethlehem.

SILENT MEDITATION

Leader — We add to Mary's meditation our own inner prayers of silence and gratitude. *(After a period of silence, the leader goes on.)*

CONCLUDING PRAYERS

Leader — "Lord, teach us to pray," asked the disciples. As we enjoy the celebration of our Lord's birth, so give us enthusiasm for his Gospel—expressed in the prayer that Jesus taught us to pray. Let us now—imagining, for the moment, the infinite God as a father—recite "the Lord's prayer."

All — Our Father, who art in heaven, hallowed be thy name, etc.

Leader — May the Holy Spirit of God bless us with joy so that we may be a blessing to those near us and all of our race who are in greatest need. May the historical coming of the Messiah inspire us in our own messianic mission—to build the reign and justice of God on earth everywhere.

All — Amen.

NEW OPENNESS
Forgive Us Our Debts
Psalm of Forgiveness

CALL TO WORSHIP

Leader   May the Spirit of God be with you.

All   And also with you.

Leader   Open our hearts, Holy Spirit, to all you would have us know and feel.

All   Amen.

ANTIPHONAL PSALM
*(Group A—or Leader—reads **bold** lines. The others read regular lines.)*

Holy Being who created and creates us
    who looks on us this day with love
    who stands under and understands, all that is, seen and unseen
    We cannot begin to pay our debts to you
        so please *forgive* us, will you, all our debts. . . ?
    Thus your prophet, Jesus, taught us to pray:
        "Forgive us our trespasses, our debts."

    Whatever is good around us or within us
    whatever is promising and awesomely wonderful
    whatever gives us delight and foreshadows our eternal destiny of joy
    whatever we have or hope to have
    we are *indebted* to you for, Divine Spirit

Forgive us, then, those debts—as we forgive *our* debtors. . .
    For there *are* people who are *our* debtors,
        who do stand indebted to us
    people we've enriched or cared for or helped—who have forgotten us
    or people who have taken what is ours or offended us unjustly
    or people who look down on us as evil or as less than themselves

    Apart from the public forum—in the personal forum
        we forgive them their debts to us
        despite our contrary feelings, we do wipe away their debts
        and do not ask them to ever pay them to us, no matter how large

Thus we know you will forgive us our even greater debts to you
    And we ask to stand with you against all long-harbored ill will
        all hatred, all vengeance,
    and in favor of mercy rather than retribution

May we have the faith to understand evil as you do
> as part of ourselves, part of our life
> but with you endurable, even manageable

because with you we are empowered
> to struggle against all that diminishes our lives
> and the lives of those we love.

Vengeance, revenge, reprisal, retribution, getting even
> **paying back an evil for an evil**

our world is full of such, our culture is sick with it
> **styles of life that make our earthly companions our enemies**
> **that make us into manipulators instead of listeners**

that turn so many refreshing experiences sour
and make us either hate opponents who are really full of beauty
> **or worship what is only superficial and illusory**

Give us the gracefulness, O Greatest Beauty,
to love what is beautiful,
to admire what is generous
to hate only what is destructive, cruel, separating and disempowering
to accept into the human family, in some way, every last member,
> forgiving them their debts
> since we ask You also to forgive us our debts of gratitude to you
> infinite beyond measure. Amen.

RELATED GOSPEL READING
Luke 6:32-38   Jesus speaks of forgiveness and tolerance.

SILENT MEDITATION

Leader   We give thanks now in silence for all we have been forgiven. *(After a period of silence, the leader goes on.)*

CONCLUDING PRAYERS

Leader   Let us now recite the prayer that the Lord Jesus taught them, imagining God as our father in heaven.

All   Our Father, who art in heaven, hallowed be thy name, etc.

Leader   May the holy presence of God fill us with the spirit of forgiveness, and show us how to find the beauty in others which reflects the divine beauty itself, hidden though it may be. May our empowerment to struggle against evil help us to be forgiving. And may God bless us with eyes to see what is hidden, and ears to hear God's song in the silence of faith.

All   Amen.

JOY IN CHRIST
All the Earth Is His Nation
from Psalm 72

CALL TO WORSHIP

Leader   May the love of God and peace of Christ be with you.

All   And also with you.

Leader   Spirit of God, we thank you for the coming of the Christ, for the wisdom of his Gospel, and the joy of his companionship.

All   Amen.

ANTIPHONAL PSALM
*(Group A—or Leader—reads **bold** lines. The others read regular lines.)*

Gracious God, may our Sovereign bring justice
May Messiah bring swift liberation
  May he reverence and cherish your people
  Bringing honor and peace to the desperate
    Even mountains and hills will be fruitful
    Bearing joy for all suffering people
      Our King will defend all the poorest
      Our King will defeat all oppressors

While the sun and the moon last in heaven
So lasting will be the king's splendor
  And as welcome as rain on the pasture
  Will he be to our thirst and despairing
    In his reign worthy labors will flourish
    And his peace last as long as the heavens
      And his song ring from ocean to ocean
      From this place to the ends of creation

Kings of the world shall respect him
Of Tarshish, the Isles and of Sheba
  All lords of Arabia also:
  All the earth is his nation and kingdom

He'll rescue the poor in their anguish
The afflicted with no one to help them
He'll have a true heart for the lowly
And the lands of the poor he'll recover

Gracious God, may our Sovereign bring justice
May Messiah bring swift liberation

RELATED GOSPEL READING
Luke 6:17-26 Jesus tells the Good News to his followers.

SILENT MEDITATION

Leader We now listen in silence to what the Messiah says in our hearts. *(After a period of silence, the leader goes on.)*

CONCLUDING PRAYERS

Leader Lord Jesus, teach us to pray with all our hearts in the words you gave to your own disciples when they asked how to pray.

All Our Father, who art in heaven, hallowed be thy name, etc.

Leader May the God of Love enlighten us with the Good News of the Messiah: of how much God cares for the world, of how precious is each least of Christ's brothers and sisters, and of how the cross is sometimes the way of liberation. Let us see the world with ever new eyes, and offer ourselves daily to service in God's New City.

All Thanks be to God.

TIME FOR JOY
Let All the World Sing
Psalm of Joy

CALL TO WORSHIP
Leader   May the Spirit of God be with you.

All   And also with you.

Leader   May our prayers together today, dear God of Mystery, be like a song, harmonized, human: the artistry of plain people seeking you together. In the spirit of humility and honesty we simply come before you, knowing our good intentions are themselves fervent prayers and our needs eloquent words in your sight.

All   Amen.

ANTIPHONAL PSALM
*(Group A—or Leader—reads **bold** lines. The others read regular lines.)*

Let all the world sing out to God with joy
white antelopes, great trees and burning stars,
oceans of space, tall mountains, thunderheads,
magnetic clouds and crimson mists of Mars.

    Let all the earth cry out to God with joy,
    Whatever's underground or grows as grain,
    All solids, liquids, gases, vacuums, space,
    All colors of the crystal or the rain.

Let all the world sing out to God with joy
All beats, vibrations, undulations, waves,
All sounds from wind or earthquake or typhoon,
All echos out of valleys, cliffs or caves.

    Let all the earth cry out to God with joy
    Except those humans who reject their home,
    Who've chosen isolation as their name,
    With sightless eyes of glass and hearts of stone.

Let all the world sing out to God with joy
for all we see and all we do not know,
For all who trust creation thank our God,
the mystery from whom all blessings flow.

RELATED GOSPEL READING
Matthew 2:1-12 Matthew describes the visit of the Magi to the child.

SILENT MEDITATION

Leader   For a few minutes in silence, ask for the gift of prayer and an understanding of the Gospel. *(After a period of silence, the leader goes on.)*

CONCLUDING PRAYERS

Leader   We learn to pray from Jesus. Let us now recite the prayer that the Lord Jesus taught, imagining God as a perfect father.

All   Our Father, who art in heaven, hallowed be thy name, etc.

Leader   Gather together, Divine Parent of us all, the simple, sacred toys of our ordinary words and thoughts, the playthings that are our joys and the puzzles of our concerns. Put them away for the moment with affectionate care. Move us on now into the more serious events of our spiritual childhood—our communications with you—for we know that all we do and say, endure and desire are precious in your sight.

All   Blest be God forever.

TRANSPARENT TO GOD
Look Into the Soul
Psalm in Silence

	CALL TO WORSHIP
Leader	May the God who loves justice be with you.
All	And also with you.
Leader	Let us pray this psalm in the silence of our hearts. *(If all do not have a copy, Leader says: "We open our hearts to this meditation before the face of God present among us and within us." Then the Leader reads.)*

Look into the soul of my soul, All-knowing, Loving Creator
See the heart of my heart
See my face behind my face:
Before you is the real me that even I don't know as you do
   but want to be known
   and enjoy being known
     by you

In the soul of my soul you see my goodness
   and would I not be quite surprised were I to see it myself
   with a beauty to match a color-flashing star
   a little less than an angel
   a wonder of an immortal person
     more substantial than any mountain or ocean
     more gifted and lifed
       than my brother orchids and uncle banyan trees
       than my sister leopards and my marvelous cousin bees

And in the heart of my heart
   you see how I long for you
     and for all the community and enlightenment I was made for
   you see in my heart those I love and those I fear and envy
     as I never can see them:
I am glad Someone sees my heart,
   someone greater than my heart

But mostly see my real face, Holy Love
   not the face I can manage this moment
   not the face I see in the mirror of my enemies' eyes
   not the face disfigured by egotism or habits of isolation

**nor any of the masks I enjoy wearing when I am on stage
or the face-protected helmet I wear into battle
but see my real face here beneath it all: my *self*
the self that surrenders to you this moment
to your way, to your plans, to your view of everything
and rejoices to be known**

**See me to my core, Creator Parent
who imagined, then designed, then uttered *me*
Enjoy my childish talk and purposeful vulnerability
Study what you have woven together
what you have shaped and decorated
and so often repaired and healed
And smile on the work of your hands**

RELATED GOSPEL READING
Mark 1:35 Jesus prays alone in the early morning.

SILENT MEDITATION

Leader — For a few minutes in silence, we ask for the gift of "a heart skilled in listening." We present ourselves to God both personally and as part of a community of faith. *(After a period of silence, the leader goes on.)*

CONCLUDING PRAYERS

Leader — Lord, teach us to pray. Hear our prayer now as we recite the prayer which the Lord Jesus taught to us, imagining the infinite God as a good father to us.

All — Our Father, who art in heaven, hallowed be thy name, etc.

Leader — Dear God, you know each of us so well, all the minutes and seconds of our earthly lives thus far, all the heights and depths of our joys and sorrows. We rest now in your knowledge of us, trusting that you give meaning to it all, to every event, to every mistake, to every disappointment, to every desire. And this awareness we have gives us joy and gratitude and trust.

All — Blest be God forever.

DARK DAYS
Why Have You Forsaken Me?
from Psalm 22

CALL TO WORSHIP
Leader   May the Spirit of God be with you.

All   And also with you.

Leader   Holy Creator God, help us pray today as Christ did on the cross—in honest anguish and bewilderment, yet with a persevering faith. As he found in the psalms words for his feelings, so may we pray those same psalms in times of distress and despair.

All   Amen.

ANTIPHONAL PSALM
*(Group A—or Leader—reads **bold** lines. The others read regular lines.)*

My God, my God, why have you forsaken me?
>My God, my God, why have you abandoned me?

All who see me scoff at me
they mock me with their lips, they wag their heads:
>"He trusted God, leave him to God
>let God save him if he can."

Look how many dogs surround me
a pack of evildoers closes in
>They pierce my hands and feet
>I can number all my bones

They even take my clothing for their own
they gamble for my very garments
>But you, my God, be not far from me
>O my helper, hasten to my aid

Leader	**Let us listen in silence to the voice of God in our own lives.**
	(after a period of silence)
	**As we continue the same psalm,
	now becoming hopeful, we pray that you will grace our own community, Holy Spirit, with hope beyond hope.**
	
	**I will proclaim your name to all the nations
	In the midst of the assembly I will give you praise:**
	    All who reverence God, now give God highest honor
	    House of Jacob, glorify your God forever

RELATED GOSPEL READING
John 19:22-24 Soldiers on Calvary fulfill the scriptural prophecy.

SILENT MEDITATION

Leader	Let us give a few minutes of silence to the memory of the cross. *(After a period of silence, the leader goes on.)*

CONCLUDING PRAYERS

Leader	Let us pray the prayer we have said all our lives, taught to us by Jesus and addressing God as our father.
All	Our Father, who art in heaven, hallowed be thy name, etc.
Leader	May the anguish and sufferings of all the world be known and understood by our human race, so that, while we see the world's agony as part of the continuing sufferings of Christ, we may still do everything we can to bring them to an end, and, with God's help, build an ever more communitarian and compassionate world.
All	Amen.

NEED FOR GOD
Out of the Depths
from Psalm 130

CALL TO WORSHIP

Leader The grace of our Lord Jesus Christ and the love of God and the companionship of the Holy Spirit be with you all.

All And also with you.

Leader Holy Spirit of God, teach us to pray—as you taught your prophet and our humble Lord, Jesus of Nazareth, at the feet of his parents, Mary and Joseph. As we pray the psalms he knew, may he live in our hearts and minds.

All Amen.

ANTIPHONAL PSALM
*(Group A—or Leader—reads **bold** lines. The others read regular lines.)*

Out of the depths I cry to you, O God
O God, hear my voice
> Let your ears be attentive
> to my voice in supplication

If you will count our failures, Holy One
who can stand?
> But you are rich in mercy:
> this we revere.

We trust in you, Creator
and your covenant,
> We are more full of hope
> than sentinels awaiting dawn

For with God is great mercy
with God swift liberation,
> For God will free the people
> from every evil.

RELATED GOSPEL READING
Matthew 18:12-14   Jesus speaks of the one lost sheep.

SILENT MEDITATION
Leader   In silence, let us forgive our enemies in our hearts, that all our own failings may be forgiven. *(After a period of silence, the leader goes on.)*

CONCLUDING PRAYERS
Leader   Let us now recite the prayer that our Lord Jesus taught them, imagining, for the moment, the infinite God as a father who is present to us.

All   Our Father, who art in heaven, hallowed be thy name, etc.

Leader   Bless us, Divine Spirit, so that we may see ourselves in your eyes: as beloved children and marvels of creation, cared for by an infinitely loving God. May we rise to the realization that, in your view of things, our sins are removed from us as far as East is from West, and, when we do wrong, our integrity is restored the instant we turn to you.

All   Blest be God forever.

PEACE OF MIND
Taste and See
from Psalm 34

CALL TO WORSHIP

Leader   The blessing and grace of God and of our Lord Jesus Christ be with you.

All   And also with you.

Leader   May we be empowered to seek justice, to love kindness, and to walk humbly with our God.

All   Blest be God forever.

ANTIPHONAL PSALM
*(Group A—or Leader—reads **bold** lines. The others read regular lines.)*

Taste and see that God is good, and with us everywhere
   Taste and see that God is good, and with us everywhere
This day I bless the God of all who knows my sorrow and my fear
   for in my solitary agony, I still could say: My God is here
     So turn to God with radiant face
     Let praise and courage be your prayer
     Be proud of this blest human family:
       when we seek God, our God is there
Taste and see that God is good, and with us everywhere
   Taste and see that God is good, and with us everywhere

So join in spirit with the poor, God hears the cry of the oppressed
All isolation is illusory, all solidarity is blest
     One joy, one pain fill all the earth
       for no one really lives alone
       and all injustice touches everyone
       as sure as if it were your own.
Taste and see that God is good, and with us everywhere
   Taste and see that God is good, and with us everywhere

So taste and see that God is good, despite the sorrow we may bear
for God is near to all humanity, and standing with us everywhere
> There is a Face that looks at mine
> There is a Heart that holds me dear
> In every danger or anxiety
> I still can say—My God is here

Taste and see that God is good, and with us everywhere
> Taste and see that God is good, and with us everywhere

RELATED GOSPEL READING
Luke 14:12-14   Jesus speaks of the poor.

SILENT MEDITATION

Leader   In silence let us accept into our hearts our own selves, poor and faulty as we may be. *(After a period of silence, the leader goes on.)*

CONCLUDING PRAYERS

Leader   Teach us to pray, Holy God, using the words you gave us through your son, our Lord, Jesus Christ.

All   Our Father, who art in heaven, hallowed be thy name, etc.

Leader   May our prayer be the beginning of a new dedication to seeking more justice in the real world for all God's children—beginning first with our own needy and limited selves. May God grant us the peace of soul that comes from unity with the Christ, and solidarity of heart with the oppressed of the earth.

All   Blest be God forever.

ISOLATION
Messiah, Jesus, Yeshua, Christ
Psalm in Silence

CALL TO WORSHIP

Leader   The peace and grace of God be with you.

All   And also with you.

Leader   Let us pray this psalm in the silence of our hearts. *(If all do not have a copy, Leader says: "We open our hearts to this meditation before the face of God present among us and within us." Then the Leader reads.)*

    Messiah, Jesus, Yeshua, Christ
       you invited us to pray to you
         and said you and "your Father" would somehow
           make us your dwelling place
       Be in my mind, Rabbi, Rabboni, Master
       Be on my lips, Word, Truth, Promise
       Be in my heart, my Lord, my Brother, my hero

    When I feel isolated from the community
       from the circle of my friends
       when certain important friends seem unreachable:
          live in me.
       Help me endure "distance," as painful as it is
       You must have felt it sometimes even with your mother and father
       You certainly often felt it with your disciples
    You knew that feeling, surely, with crowds slow to understand
    You experienced it, in its greatest depths, on the way to Calvary
       then in the excruciating agony of your execution
    I join now my own trivial pain with your own messianic anguish
       believing that, however little
          we all "fill up what is wanting to the sufferings of the Christ"

    Does this give *meaning* to this painful evil we call "distance"?
       In some ways, it does
       It puts order into the chaos that threatens us
          vanquishing some of its power
             in the struggle to overcome it and to cope with it

Then I recall that the sun will always break through the clouds again
    a metaphor built into the creation around me
  Daylight will gradually break into the dark sky
    and the little stars will fade as the Daystar rises at morning

Come, Daystar, Deliverer, Life-source, Messenger of Hope and Life
  In the darkness and "distance"
    I—full of faith—call upon you
  Hear my prayer.

RELATED GOSPEL READING
John 1: 1-14   John describes the mystery of the incarnation.

SILENT MEDITATION

Leader   Let us listen in silence to what the Spirit says to our hearts. *(After a period of silence, the leader goes on.)*

CONCLUDING PRAYERS

Leader   Together let us lift up our voices in the prayer that our Lord taught to all his disciples, imagining God as a divine father.

All   Our Father, who art in heaven, hallowed be thy name, etc.

Leader   Speak to us, Holy Spirit, in the events that take place around us, for as in the light we easily can see, so in the darkness make us better listeners. Give us the grace to accept the light, when it comes, with humility, and the darkness with patience and faith, remembering your intimate presence wherever we are.

All   Blest be God forever.

DAYS OF JOY AND HOPE
This Is the Day
from Psalm 118

Leader   CALL TO WORSHIP
May the grace and peace of our Lord Jesus Christ be with you all.

All   And also with you.

Leader   Spirit of Death and Life, of darkness and morning, of winter and spring, after the pattern of our Lord and Prophet Jesus of Nazareth, our faith convinces us to hope for life after death and for good to overcome every evil. Enliven that faith in our hearts today and always.

All   May God bless us with care for all, hope beyond hope, and faith that moves mountains.

ANTIPHONAL PSALM
*(Group A—or Leader—reads **bold** lines. The others read regular lines.)*

This is the day our God has made
    Let us rejoice and be glad in it

Give thanks to God for gracious goodness
for mercy and caring that endure forever
    Let the people of God all sing together:
    God's good compassion lasts forever

This is the day our God has made
    Let us rejoice and be glad in it

The strength of God's love shines like the sun
and nothing could be more glorious
    I shall not die but I shall live on
    to declare the wonderful works of God

This is the day our God has made
    Let us rejoice and be glad in it

The stone which the builders rejected
has become the cornerstone
    Our loving God has made this happen
    it is wonderful in our eyes

This is the day our God has made
   Let us rejoice and be glad in it

RELATED GOSPEL READING
Luke 12:32-34   Jesus preaches on the mount.

SILENT MEDITATION

Leader   In silence let us hear the Good News in our hearts. *(After a period of silence, the leader goes on.)*

CONCLUDING PRAYERS

Leader   The Our Father is the prayer given to us by Jesus himself. Together let us imagine God as our father, and all of us as members of one family.

All   Our Father, who art in heaven, hallowed be thy name, etc.

Leader   May the Holy Spirit of God bless all our joys, sorrows, sufferings and successes, and give us a sense of the spiritual world around us, filled with eternal life, freed finally from the threat of death and evil, and alive with promise and peace. We rejoice, dear God, with faith in your final victories, and asking only that we be guided into our own roles in your divine plan.

All   Blest be God forever.

THANKS AND PRAISE
Give Thanks to God
from Psalm 136

CALL TO WORSHIP

Leader   May the Spirit of God be with you.

All   And also with you.

Leader   Holy Spirit within us and around us, just as you have taught us through the resurrection of Jesus, that death is the doorway to eternal life, so teach us this day to give you thanks for the life we have, using the psalms that Jesus knew and loved—so that our minds and hearts may ever more resemble his.

All   Amen.

ANTIPHONAL PSALM
*(Leader—or Group A—reads **bold** lines. The others read regular lines.)*

Give thanks to God for worlds of goodness
    God's gracious love is everlasting
Give thanks to the God above all gods
    for heaven's care will never end

Give thanks to the Heart above all hearts
    God's gracious love is everlasting
God alone has made all wonders
    and heaven's care will never end

God made the sky in wondrous wisdom
    God's gracious love is everlasting
God spread out earth upon the waters
    and heaven's care will never end

God made the lights throughout the cosmos
    God's gracious love is everlasting
God made the sun to rule the daytime
    and heaven's care will never end

God's moon and stars rule over night
>God's gracious love is everlasting

God calms our fear of all our foes
>for heaven's care will never end

God's daily food feeds every life
>God's gracious love is everlasting

Give thanks to God for every gift
>for heaven's care will never end

RELATED GOSPEL READING
Luke 6:12-13 Jesus prays all night before choosing his apostles.

SILENT MEDITATION

Leader Let us take a few minutes to center ourselves, with quiet gratitude and confidence in God. *(After a period of silence, the leader goes on.)*

CONCLUDING PRAYERS

Leader "Lord, teach us to pray," asked the disciples. Imagining God as a father, let us say the prayer Jesus taught his disciples.

All Our Father, who art in heaven, hallowed be thy name, etc.

Leader May our prayers of thanksgiving and trust draw us together, knowing in our hearts that, as we are now earthly brothers and sisters, our common hope promises us a community in eternity as well. Be in our minds, Holy Spirit, and on our lips and in our hearts. With your presence to strengthen us, we believe that great things are possible.

All Blest be God forever.

GOD'S WONDERS
My Heart's Applause
Psalm of Appreciation

CALL TO WORSHIP

Leader   Grace and peace be yours from our gracious God and from the Lord Jesus Christ.

All   May God bless us with light and freedom.

Leader   Bless us, God Most High and Most Intimate, bless us with hearts and minds open to your influences, not limited by fear or arrogance, but empowered to give you praise from the heart of our being.

All   Amen.

ANTIPHONAL PSALM
*(Group A—or Leader—reads **bold** lines. The others read regular lines.)*

O God, wonder-worker of this universe and of every universe
    You have my heart's applause, O God, My God

For the wonders of the sky and the cosmos all around us
For the marvels within us, the known and the as yet unknown
    You have my heart's applause, O God, My God

For the wonders in those we love and in those we admire
For the marvels of love and of human faithfulness throughout history
    You have my heart's applause, O God, My God

For the wonders of this earth, its magnetism and all its forces
    its daily spin before the sun's bright face
    its yearly sweep around the sun
For the marvels of light, its measured unimaginable speed
    its infinite spectrum of colors, its haunting mystery
    You have my heart's applause, O God, My God

For the wonders and achievements of our human race
    and its remarkable ability to cope
        to forgive, to be patient, to believe, to keep hoping
For the marvels of human creativity and determination
    You have my heart's applause, O God, My God

For the mystery of grace and of your divine graciousness
For the marvels of human virtue, of wisdom
   of compassion, and of courage
   You have my heart's applause, O God, My God

RELATED GOSPEL READING
Mark 1:35   Jesus prays alone in the early morning.

SILENT MEDITATION

Leader   Let us simply spend a few minutes in the silent presence of God. *(After a period of silence, the leader goes on.)*

CONCLUDING PRAYERS

Leader   With hearts full of faith and appreciation, let us say the prayer given to us by the Lord Jesus.

All   Our Father, who art in heaven, hallowed be thy name, etc.

Leader   May the Holy Spirit of God bless us with the gift of contemplation, so that our hearts may respond to the wonders of our lives, and have a deep caring for our Mother Earth and all the creatures that live upon her. Enrich us, Parenting Creator, with a feeling of community with the creation around us, and a sense of responsibility for earth's well-being.

All   Amen.

LIFT YOUR EYES
Bless My Descendants
Psalm in Silence

           CALL TO WORSHIP
Leader   May the God who loves justice be with you.

All   And also with you.

Leader   Let us pray this psalm in the silence of our hearts. *(If all do not have a copy, Leader says: "We open our hearts to this meditation before the face of God present among us and within us." Then the Leader reads.)*

Bless my descendants, Parenting God
> not just what children I may have
> but all who may live or live more fully because of me

I am full of creativity, whoever I am
> As every fruit of every flower or tree
>> carries seeds full of hope and awesome design
> just so sacred is my own generativity
> just so productive is every thoughtful and honest life

Words carry on, acts of love carry on
> as every stirred pond carries ripples into history
>> and every kind gesture models kindness into the unknown

I bless my descendants, then, people I've nurtured and known and loved
> You know who they are, Creating God
> Carry my blessing to them from this place and this moment

Grant that time may heal mistakes and small-minded choices I've made
> In your mercy, wipe out my offenses
>> as the forgiving wind wipes out all marks in the desert sand
>> as compassionate rain washes away the sins of drought

I love my descendants: my friends and my children
> my customers, my students, my guests, and my clients
> my companions, my classmates, my partners, my competitors
> my circle of equals, my string of acquaintances
> my long line of helpers and those I have helped

I bless my descendants from where I am now
    and pray I may bless them
        from wherever I'll be through the whole of my future

May they prosper and live ever more fully
    ever more richly
    ever more freely
    marked in beauty just a little by me

And I bless the Creator of Creativity
    giving thanks for the joy of knowing
        how unexpectedly rich and productive
            have been the days and years of my life

RELATED GOSPEL READING
Matthew 13:44-52   Jesus speaks about the realm of heaven.

SILENT MEDITATION

Leader   For a few minutes in silence, ask for the gift of "a heart skilled in listening." Let us invite God to speak to us in this silent time. *(After a period of silence, the leader goes on.)*

CONCLUDING PRAYERS

Leader   Let us conclude our service with the prayer to God taught us by Jesus himself, imagining God as a perfect father.

All   Our Father, who art in heaven, hallowed be thy name, etc.

Leader   Lift our hearts, dear God of our Lives, by the remembrances of your goodness to us through the years. If there has been any generosity and energy in our own days, it is due to your holy presence within us and around us and in everything and everyone we have encountered. For all this we give you thanks.

All   Blest be God forever.

NEED OF GOD
Into Your Hands
from Psalm 31

CALL TO WORSHIP

Leader   May the Spirit of God be with you.

All   And also with you.

Leader   Holy Spirit of God, teach us to pray—as you taught your prophet and our Lord, Jesus of Nazareth, at the feet of his parents, Mary and Joseph. As we pray the psalms he knew, may he live in our hearts and minds.

All   Amen.

ANTIPHONAL PSALM
*(Group A—or Leader—reads **bold** lines. The others read regular lines.)*

Into your hands I commend my spirit
  for you have rescued me, faithful God
I will rejoice and be glad for your steadfast love
    Because you have seen my affliction
    You have taken heed of all my burdens

Be gracious to me, O God, for I am in distress
  my eyes are close to tears
  my soul and my body grieve
    For my life is filled with sorrow
      and my years are spent with sighing
      My strength fails because of my sadness

But still I trust in you, O Holy One
  and still I say, you are my God
My times are in your hands
    Let your face shine upon your servant
    Save me in your unfailing love

RELATED GOSPEL READING
John 18:1-5 The arrest of Jesus.

SILENT MEDITATION
Leader   In silence let us prepare ourselves for whatever may come about in our lives. *(After a period of silence, the leader goes on.)*

CONCLUDING PRAYERS
Leader   Together let us recite the prayer given us by Jesus, approaching God as children speaking to a loving father.

All   Our Father, who art in heaven, hallowed be thy name, etc.

Leader   May the Holy Spirit of God bless us with unshakeable faith, and give us the enrichment of a community where our experiences can be communal, and all our dreams and beliefs shared. Grant, dear God, that in the circle of our friends and family we may have strength to endure our sufferings so that we may share in the glory of the resurrection.

All   Amen.

WELCOMING GOD
Send Forth Your Spirit
from Psalm 104

CALL TO WORSHIP

Leader   The grace and peace of God and of the Lord Jesus Christ be with you.

All   And also with you.

Leader   Holy Spirit of God, so silent that we sometimes forget your presence, so invisible that we can imagine we are alone, open our ears and eyes to the evidence of your actions in our hearts and throughout the universe.

All   Come, Holy Spirit, come.

ANTIPHONAL PSALM
(Group A—or Leader—reads bold lines. The others read regular lines.)

Send forth your spirit, God, create new wonders
Come, Wind and Fire, give everything new birth
     So born again of water and your Spirit
     We celebrate your coming to the earth

Around us everywhere, O God, are creatures
Your countless living things, both great and small
Your handiwork exquisitely invented
In wisdom and delight you made them all
     Inhabit they the earth and ocean waters
     With ships above and whales at sport below
     Each creature looks to you for food in season
     You open up your hand and all things grow

Send forth your spirit, God, create new wonders
Come, Wind and Fire, give everything new birth
     So born again of water and your Spirit
     We celebrate your coming to the earth

Things come to life when you breathe forth your Spirit
In springtime earth will dance in green attire
The hills will move each time you look upon them
You touch the mountaintops and they catch fire

>   Yes I will sing to God a song of wonder
>   And praise the Spirit of my life in song
>   Come, Holy One, and hear my admiration
>   Rejoicing in your love my whole life long
>
> **Send forth your spirit, God, create new wonders**
> **Come, Wind and Fire, give everything new birth**
>
>   > So born again of water and your Spirit
>   > We celebrate your coming to the earth

RELATED GOSPEL READING
John 14:16-17   Jesus promises the Paraclete.

SILENT MEDITATION

Leader   For a few minutes of silence let us welcome the Paraclete into our own hearts. *(After a period of silence, the leader goes on.)*

CONCLUDING PRAYERS

Leader   With the confidence of children approaching a kindly parent, let us say the prayer given to us by Jesus.

All   Our Father, who art in heaven, hallowed be thy name, etc.

Leader   Come, Holy Spirit, illuminate the hearts of your faithful, and enkindle in us the fire of your love.

All   Send forth your Spirit—as you renew the face of the earth.

Leader   May the gracious inspirations of God fill us with the courage and energy for a more fulfilled and more useful life. Come, Holy Spirit of Creativity, of Caring, of Wisdom, of Mystery, fill our hearts with faith and our lives with the courage of our convictions.

All   Blest be God forever.

REMEMBERING WELL
In Memory of You
Psalm of Silence

Leader   CALL TO WORSHIP
May the God who loves justice be with you.

All   And also with you.

Leader   Let us pray this psalm in the silence of our hearts. *(If all do not have a copy, Leader says: "We open our hearts to this meditation before the face of God present among us and within us." Then the Leader reads.)*

All praise to you, Messiah, Jesus of Nazareth
    Prophet of a New Covenant, Bearer of Good News
       who rescues your disciples from blindness and egotism
    We live "in memory of " you
       especially of the day before your execution
"This is my body" you said of the bread
    Then you broke it and gave it away
       with the words: do *this* in memory of me
Give our bodies away, shared—in memory of you?
Give whatever we have—in memory of how you did the same?
Our days of care and work? Our nights of searching? Our midnights of faith?
Give away our heart's caring, our mind's strength, our pain, our delights?
Give all?
"This cup is a new covenant in my blood," you said.
The communal cup is a new covenant?

A circle of disciples, drinking from a cup together
    is a new covenant? with *God*?
        a covenant created in your blood, in your last step
           into solidarity with the oppressed?

    Perhaps we should share such a cup more often
        linking ourselves together more often
           in that common dream
        a faith in an unseen world of divine covenant
           and earthly communion

We praise you, Messiah, Jesus of Nazareth
    We live in memory of you

RELATED GOSPEL READING
Matthew 25:31-41   Jesus tells the parable of the last judgment.

SILENT MEDITATION

Leader For a few minutes in silence, consider the presence of God and the desires of your own heart. *(After a period of silence, the leader goes on.)*

CONCLUDING PRAYERS

Leader "Teach us to pray, Lord," asked the disciples. Let us now recite the prayer that the Lord Jesus gave his followers, imagining the infinite God as our heavenly father.

All Our Father, who art in heaven, hallowed be thy name, etc.

Leader Most Compassionate Spirit, Creator and Sustainer of Life and of all that is, we choose not to offend you by fearing you or your judgments of us. But we are in awe, dear God, at your ways: Are our simple achievements acceptable to you? Are our distracted lives satisfactory in your sight? Our faith tells us they are. Help us ever to grow in faith and the lightheartedness of those who believe deeply in your all-compassionate Love.

All Blest be God forever.

TRUST IN GOD
My Light and My Hope
from Psalm 27

CALL TO WORSHIP

Leader   The Spirit of God be with you always.

All   And also with you.

Leader   Dear God, though dangers lie all around us, we shall not fear. Give us words to speak to you, as children speak confidently to their parents and friends speak easily with each other.

All   Blest be God forever.

ANTIPHONAL PSALM
*(Group A—or Leader—reads **bold** lines. The others read regular lines.)*

The Spirit is my light and my hope
  whom shall I fear?
The Giver of Life
  is the stronghold of my days
  Of whom shall I be afraid?

> One thing have I asked of our God, that will I seek
> to dwell at the heart of God's family
> all the days of my life
> to see before me the divine beauty
> and cherish God's holy temple

For God will hide me in the day of trouble
  and conceal me in perfect care
  and set me on a safe high place
  where I will sing
  and make melodies of praise

> Hear me, Holy One, when I cry aloud
> be gracious to me and answer me
> You have said
> Seek a place before my face

My heart replies:
   Your face, my God, I do seek
   Hide not your face from me
   For, though my father and mother may forsake me
   You, Holy One, will take me up
> Teach me your ways, my God
>   and lead me on a level path
> I believe that I shall see the goodness of God
>   in the land of life

RELATED GOSPEL READING
Luke 17:11-19   Jesus heals ten persons afflicted with leprosy.

SILENT MEDITATION

Leader   Let us turn to God with our own inner psalm of silence and gratitude. *(After a period of silence, the leader goes on.)*

CONCLUDING PRAYERS

Leader   We learned from our Lord that we may approach God as children approach in confidence their loving parent. We recite the Lord's prayer with our hearts united.

All   Our Father, who art in heaven, hallowed be thy name, etc.

Leader   Bless us, dear God, with the energy to promote your reign as Sovereign among us, so that we can delight in freedom from fear and dedication to your ways. Your love, Holy One, is our heart's home, and we are restless until we rest in you. Keep us in your love.

All   Blest be God forever.

DESIRE TO SERVE
If Today You Hear God's Voice
from Psalm 95

	CALL TO WORSHIP
Leader	The love of God and of our Lord Jesus Christ be with you all.
All	And also with you.
Leader	Divine Spirit, draw us into your light, illuminate our minds with a knowledge of you, and give us energy to search for you where you can be found: first in the pursuit of justice, and then in the light of prayer.
All	May the Divine Presence fill our minds and our hearts.

ANTIPHONAL PSALM
*(Group A—or Leader—reads **bold** lines. The others read regular lines.)*

Come, sing together joy in God
    And greet our Rock of life and peace
Seek God's face with songs of thanks
    For the One who gives the earth increase

    If today you hear God's voice
        harden not your heart, but be aware
    And turn your face to those in need
        the Voice and Cry and Call of God is there

Come, bow before the Source of Life
    Come, kneel before our gracious God
For Earth's Creator is our All
    Who shepherds us with staff and rod

    If today you hear God's voice
        harden not your heart, but be aware
    And turn your face to those in need
        the Voice and Cry and Call of God is there

If today you hear God's voice
Turn not your heart and face away
As at Meribah, in the desert of Massah
There where your kin once lost their way

> If today you hear God's voice
> > harden not your heart, but be aware
> And turn your face to those in need
> > the Voice and Cry and Call of God is there

RELATED GOSPEL READING
Matthew 25:34-40   Jesus and the poor judge the world.

SILENT MEDITATION

Leader In silence let us ask God to lead us wisely in serving the needs of those around us. *(After a period of silence, the leader goes on.)*

CONCLUDING PRAYERS

Leader "Lord, teach us to pray," asked the disciples. Let us now recite the prayer that the Lord Jesus taught them, imagining, for the moment, the infinite God as a father.

All Our Father, who art in heaven, hallowed be thy name, etc.

Leader Dear Parenting Spirit, unthreatening and liberating, we thank you for all you have done for us, especially for the constant joy of knowing you are present, with us, in us and around us. Teach us to be, like you, present to those who need us and who depend on us. Help us to accept our limitations, and to learn, with the help of others, what is our small part of the world's work.

All Blest be God forever.

ACCEPTANCE
Praise God for Our Enemies
Psalm of Trust

CALL TO WORSHIP

Leader   May the Spirit of God be with you.

All   And also with you.

Leader   Holy Spirit of God, teach us to pray—as you taught your prophet and our Lord, Jesus of Nazareth, at the feet of his parents, Mary and Joseph. As we learn to pray, may Jesus live in our hearts and minds, so we may establish the reign of God in our own hearts and throughout the world.

All   Blest be God forever.

ANTIPHONAL PSALM
*(Group A—or Leader—reads **bold** lines. The others read regular lines.)*

We praise you, Holy God, for our enemies
    for your steadfast love endures forever
We praise you in all our defeats
    for heaven's care will have no end
We praise you in our sorrows
    for your steadfast love endures forever
And we praise you amidst our mourning
    for heaven's care will have no end

     We can't understand the shadows around us
       or the never-ending victories of death and evil
         of pain and separation and failure
       or the betrayal of agreement and promise
     But you stand at our side whatever befalls
       and we praise your mysteries of presence and absence

Yes, we observe even your apparent absence
    for you seem to make no sound or movement
      that would tell us you are here
We look for you, listen for you, in churches empty or full
    yet we are left with only our faith

We praise you, Holy God, for our enemies
   for your steadfast love endures forever
We praise you in all our defeats
   for heaven's care will have no end
We praise you in our sorrows
   for your steadfast love endures forever
And we praise you amidst our mourning
   for heaven's care will have no end

RELATED GOSPEL READING
Matthew 18:21-35 Jesus tells a parable of the realm of heaven.

SILENT MEDITATION

Leader   For a few minutes in silence, ask for the gift of "a heart skilled in listening." Our silence speaks of our faith, and God's silence speaks a mystery beyond sound or imagination. *(After a period of silence, the leader goes on.)*

CONCLUDING PRAYERS

Leader   Let us begin our concluding prayers with the Our Father, which was taught us by our Lord, Jesus himself, addressing the infinite God under the image of a loving father.

All   Our Father, who art in heaven, hallowed be thy name, etc.

Leader   God of All, even your greatest mysteries do not shatter our faith. We are your servants, your children, your creations. We give you thanks that we have made it through the paths of life thus far, and with your help and wonderful presence, we shall arrive successfully at our journey's end, in the company of those we love.

All   Blest be God forever.

FOLLOWING CHRIST
Make Us Disciples
A Psalm of Devotion

CALL TO WORSHIP

Leader   May the grace and fellowship of the Lord Jesus be yours.

All   May God grant us the grace to know, love, and serve the Christ with all our hearts.

Leader   Good Spirit, in and beyond all creation, guide our minds and hearts along the Way taught by Jesus of Nazareth.

All   Come, Holy Spirit, fill the hearts of your faithful, and enkindle in us the fire of love. Send forth your Spirit and we shall be as if born again with energy for each day's messianic task. Amen.

ANTIPHONAL PSALM
*(Group A—or Leader—reads **bold** lines. The others read regular lines.)*

Make us disciples, Loving Spirit
   make us disciples of the Christ you sent us so many years ago
Thus may we fulfill Christ's dreams with everything we do
   from our awakening in the morning
   to our prayers, our enjoyments, our conversations, our work
   our patience, our industry, our forgiveness, and our courage
   and "fill up" in our own lives "what is wanting" to his
     he *in us* and our community
     and all of us *in him*

   Jesus, live! So live in me
     that all I do be done by thee
   And grant that all I think and say
     may be thy thought and word today

Guide our minds and hearts, gracious Spirit
   through the study of the Gospels
   to "put on Christ" like our truest garment
   preferring what he preferred, loving what he cared about
   trusting what he trusted, following the Way he went

Jesus, live! So live in me
> that all you'd feel be felt by me
And grant that all you'd sing or say
> may be my song and word today

Thus may we become our truest selves as he was uniquely himself
> **multiplying the messianic impulse**
>> **to live a full and caring life**
>> **to rescue the world from illusion and isolation**
>> **to build God's sovereign reign**
>> **to be worshippers of the true God**
>>> **and good stewards of our earthly home**
>>> **diligent workers at this world's projects**
>>> **healers of this world's wounded**
>> **and believer-enactors of the weightier things of the Law:**
>>> **right judgment, mercy, faith**

Jesus, live and pray in me
> that my poor prayers be prayed by thee
And grant that all you'd have me say
> May be my humble prayer today

RELATED GOSPEL READING
Luke 5:1-11   Peter, James, and John become disciples.

SILENT MEDITATION

Leader Dear Lord, let us hear your call in the silence, let us see your face in the darkness. *(After a period of silence, the leader goes on.)*

CONCLUDING PRAYERS

Leader We bring our prayers to an end, reciting the prayer given to us by our Lord, Jesus, when asked by his disciples to teach them how to pray.

All Our Father, who art in heaven, hallowed be thy name, etc.

Leader May the Holy Spirit of God bless us with perseverance in our calling, whatever that may be or become. Parenting Creator, enrich us with devotion to our part of the work of Christ and of the inevitable victory of justice and peace.

All Amen.

LOVE FOR GOD
Bless Your God
from Psalm 103

CALL TO WORSHIP

Leader   The love of God be with you all.

All   And also with you.

Leader   Holy Spirit of God, teach us to pray—as you taught your prophet and our Lord, Jesus of Nazareth, at the feet of his parents, Mary and Joseph. As we pray the prayers he knew, may he live in our hearts and minds.

All   Amen.

ANTIPHONAL PSALM
*(Group A—or Leader—reads **bold** lines. The others read regular lines.)*

Bless your God, O my soul
and let all that is within me bless God's holy name

    Bless your God, O my soul
    and forget not all God's blessings

For God forgives all your faults
and heals all your diseases

    God removes the fear of death
    and crowns you with steadfast love

God satisfies you with good things
as long as you live

    so that your youth is renewed
    made new like the eagle's

God works liberation and justice
for all who are oppressed

    God made known the right path to Moses
    and was gracious to the people of Israel

God is full of mercy and generosity
forgiving and full of care

    God does not deal with us according to our sins
    nor repay us according to our failures

**For as the sky is high above the earth
so great does God's love tower over us**
> And as far as east is from the west
> so far does God remove our sins from us

**As parents pity their own children
   so God has pity on the faithful**
> Bless your God, O my soul
> and let all that is within me bless God's holy name

RELATED GOSPEL READING
Luke 4:14-21   Jesus preaches in his hometown synagogue.

SILENT MEDITATION

Leader   In silence let us open ourselves to God's call to us personally. *(After a period of silence, the leader goes on.)*

CONCLUDING PRAYERS

Leader   "Lord, teach us to pray," asked the disciples. Let us now recite the prayer to God as father, given to us by Jesus himself.

All   Our Father, who art in heaven, hallowed be thy name, etc.

Leader   Dear God, present to all our comings and goings, all our thoughts and dreams, all our triumphs and defeats, give us renewed confidence in your care so we may find comfort in you in all life's crises. We are before you in humble discipleship and willingness. Enter and take possession of our hearts.

All   Amen.

KEEPING FAITH
Creation's Composer
Psalm of Confidence

CALL TO WORSHIP

Leader   May the peace of God be with you.

All   And also with you.

Leader   O God, who hears every prayer even before we utter the words, guide us on our journey of prayer today—that our mind may be full of faith seeking understanding.

All   Blest be God forever.

ANTIPHONAL PSALM
*(Group A—or Leader—reads **bold** lines. The others read regular lines.)*

Creation's Composer, inventor of all that is
    its amazing rhythm, harmony, melody and sound
    all matter and energy, its meaning and poetry, tempo and dynamics
    pitch and key, sequence, rhyme, vibration and style
give us an ear for your music
    the mysterious music of earth, of sun, of galaxy and cosmos
    and the delicate swift melodies of pulsing waves of light
        the rhythms in atoms and cells electric with energy
        of magnetic masses and forces not yet named
        the variations of life forms almost infinite in number
            and all evolving improvisations
give us the steadfastness to hear the cosmic composition to the finish
    keeping faith
    keeping hope
        that the final notes will make a symphony of it all

And may each of us be and become our musical part
    a song, a hymn, a solo, or an accompaniment—but always a part
    a melody of meaning set to our own unique rhythms
        beginning at a certain instant in time
        and growing more distinctive as our beat goes on
    repeating, innovating, emphasizing, quickening, pausing:
        true to our musical purpose—foreseen and known only to the composer
            understood only at the end

RELATED GOSPEL READING
Matthew 22:34-40 Jesus describes the two great commandments.

SILENT MEDITATION
Leader   We add to Mary's canticle our own inner psalm of silence and gratitude. *(After a period of silence, the leader goes on.)*

CONCLUDING PRAYERS
Leader   "Lord, teach us to pray," asked the disciples. Let us now recite the prayer that the Lord Jesus taught them, imagining, for the moment, the infinite God as a father.

All   Our Father, who art in heaven, hallowed be thy name, etc.

Leader   May God enlighten us to endure the sorrows of our life with patience and faith, and see our joys as sacraments and promises of the victory of good over evil, and life over death. May we live with faith in God and faith in ourselves as well, remembering that a most Creative Composer invented us, and we are perfectly made for our purpose in the symphony.

All   Blest be God forever.

RELYING ON GOD
Come, Hear My Prayer
from Psalm 17

CALL TO WORSHIP
Leader   May the Spirit of God be with you.

All   And also with you.

Leader   Divine Spirit, teach us how to trust that you care for us infinitely, and that the ends of the earth are in your caring hands.

All   Amen.

ANTIPHONAL PSALM
*(Group A—or Leader—reads **bold** lines. The others read regular lines.)*

Come, hear my prayer, my God, attend my cry
   Come, give me your compassion in my need
From you alone my hope of victory comes
   Look on your child who turns in hope to you
      You know, dear God, my present and my past
      I trust in you as long as life shall last

If you can see my heart, you know my needs
   if you visit me by night, you know my dreams
If you should test me, I will not betray you
   and you will find no lack of faith in me
      You know, dear God, my present and my past
      I trust in you as long as life shall last

My mouth speaks truth and ever is forgiving
   and I avoid the ways of violence
My steps have followed faithfully your paths
   my feet have never slipped along the way
      You know, dear God, my present and my past
      I trust in you as long as life shall last

I call on you, my God, for you will answer
  Turn your ear to me and hear my words
Wonderfully show your steadfast care
  For you will save all those who turn to you
    You know, dear God, my present and my past
    I trust in you as long as life shall last

Guard me as the apple of your eye
  and hide me in the shadow of your wings
Come hear my prayer, my God, attend my cry
  Come, give me your compassion in my need
    You know, dear God, my present and my past
    I trust in you as long as life shall last

RELATED GOSPEL READING
Luke 9:57-58   Jesus describes his life of trust.

SILENT MEDITATION

Leader   Let us consider, for a few moments of silence, the lifestyle of Jesus of Nazareth. *(After a period of silence, the leader goes on.)*

CONCLUDING PRAYERS

Leader   When the disciples asked, "Lord, teach us to pray," Jesus gave them the prayer we know as the Our Father. Let us now pray that prayer, imagining, for the moment, the infinite God as a father.

All   Our Father, who art in heaven, hallowed be thy name, etc.

Leader   Praise and thanksgiving to the God who fills our lives with blessings of every kind, and who never abandons us in our neediness and suffering. Give us the wisdom, Holy God, never to despair, for, like Christ, we want to be your servants through all of life's mysterious ups and downs.

All   Amen.

CLOSENESS TO GOD
My Soul Longs for You
from Psalm 63

CALL TO WORSHIP

Leader   May the Spirit of God be with you.

All   And also with you.

Leader   Holy Spirit of God, teach us to pray—as you taught your prophet and our humble Lord, Jesus of Nazareth, at the feet of his parents. As we pray the psalms he knew, may he live in our hearts and minds.

All   Amen.

ANTIPHONAL PSALM
*(Group A—or Leader—reads **bold** lines. The others read regular lines.)*

My soul longs for you, O God, my God!
    My soul longs for you, O God, my God!

O God, you are the God whom I do seek
For you my body pines, my soul's in pain
    Like earth herself when parched and deep in dust
    Like earth herself when rivers long for rain

    My soul longs for you, O God, my God

Thus have I sought your sanctuary's glow
And feel your awesomeness in all I see
    For your kind presence is more dear than life
    And while I can, my lips shall sing of thee

    My soul longs for you, O God, my God

You are my help, my refuge, and my God
The shadow of your wings: my hope and cheer
    My soul clings fast to you, my God and All
    Your presence gives me life and calms my fear

    My soul longs for you, O God, my God

you all the days I live
ds, and all your honors sing
st will then its hunger fill
quenched at your fresh-flowing spring.

ongs for you, O God, my God

SPEL READING
5 Jesus says goodbye to his followers.

DITATION

Leader   let us think about what the Christ asks of us. *(After a period of silence, the leader goes on.)*

CONCLUDING PRAYERS

Leader   Our Lord, Jesus Christ, gave his disciples a lesson in prayer when they requested it. Let us say that prayer together, imagining God as a father.

All   Our Father, who art in heaven, hallowed be thy name, etc.

Leader   May the Holy Spirit of God bless all our joys, sorrows, sufferings and successes, and give us a sense of the spiritual world around us, and the importance of one another in the eyes of God. May God grant us hearts like Christ's and minds open to the desires of the just and loving God within and around us.

All   Amen.

HONESTY WITH GOD
How We Do Blunder
Psalm of Honesty

CALL TO WORSHIP

Leader   May the Spirit of God guard your hearts unto eternal life.

All   We turn our hearts toward the face of God.

Leader   O God, who hears every prayer even before we utter the words, guide us on our journey of prayer today—that our mind may be full of faith seeking understanding, and our hearts rich in the realism of honest humility.

All   Amen.

ANTIPHONAL PSALM
*(Group A—or Leader—reads **bold** lines. The others read regular lines.)*

How we do blunder, O God beyond us and before us
  within us and around us
> How we do blunder and stumble and go astray
>   in our attempts to reach toward you
>   and walk toward you together

How we do stone to death your true prophets
  and make idols to worship out of lifeless clay and ore
> How we do enjoy illusions of light when such are convenient
>   and prefer the dreamworld of acting "as if"
>   to the real world of ambiguity and honest doubt
>   and frank, risk-taking communication

Cure us, Healing Presence, of our false prudence
  and our timidity
> Gift us with courage equal to the task
>   of being and becoming ourselves in community
>   the selves we are and were meant to live out
>   our best selves, our authentic selves, our true selves
>   not any false, distorted, illusory, lesser self

That is the self you like best, Gracious God
—no, rather, that is the *only* self you can see or care about
since it is our only real self
all others are illusory, unreal and false

> Our best self, our real self, greets you, Great Intimate Reality
> and we know our greeting means a great deal to you
> > as every mother's joy is the voice of her child
> > and potters' hearts rise at the sight of their handiwork

RELATED GOSPEL READING
Matthew 6:19-21   Jesus shares his wisdom.

SILENT MEDITATION

Leader   Let us silently reach toward the Wisdom that is God. *(After a period of silence, the leader goes on.)*

CONCLUDING PRAYERS

Leader   "Lord, teach us to pray," asked the disciples. Then they listened and Jesus taught them the Our Father. Let us say the prayer together as disciples of Jesus also.

All   Our Father, who art in heaven, hallowed be thy name, etc.

Leader   Give us always, Holy One, the grace of Wisdom and Honesty, so we may be and become disciples of Jesus of Nazareth, our Messiah. And may the blessing of the All-compassionate God, the wisdom of our Messiah, and community in the Holy Spirit be ours today and forever.

All   Amen.

CARING FOR EARTH
I Will Praise Your Name
from Psalm 145

CALL TO WORSHIP

Leader   The grace and peace of God be with you all.

All   And also with you.

Leader   Holy Creating Love, surrounding us with mystery, open our eyes to the beauty and fragility of the earth home you have given us—a globe teeming with life spinning around a fiery star. As our hearts go out first to the most needy of our human race, so may they open to our responsibility to the needs of all living things and all creation, radically threatened by our abuse of the earth.

All   Amen.

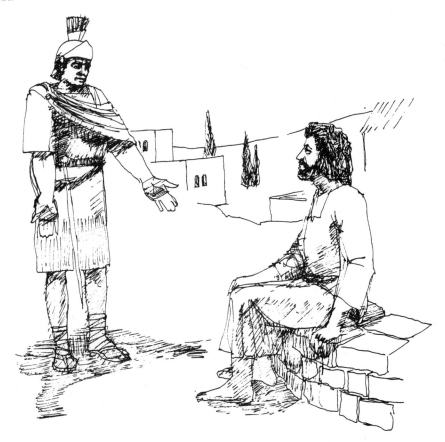

ANTIPHONAL PSALM
*(Group A—or Leader—reads **bold** lines. The others read regular lines.)*

**I will praise your name forever, my Sovereign and my God
and I will bless your name all my days**
> Every day I will exalt you
> and I will honor your faithfulness without ceasing

**Our God is gracious and merciful
generous in judgment and of great kindness**
> Our God is good to all
> and compassionate toward all creation

**Let your works give you thanks, O God
and let your faithful ones bless you**
> Let them sing of the glory of your kindness
> and speak of your awesome ways.

**Our God is faithful in every word
and holy in every work**
> Our God lifts up all who are falling
> and raises up all who are bowed down

RELATED GOSPEL READING
Luke 7:1-10 Jesus heals the slave of a centurion.

SILENT MEDITATION

Leader Let us take a time for silent prayer, asking for inner healing. *(After a period of silence, the leader goes on.)*

CONCLUDING PRAYERS

Leader Jesus taught his disciples to pray to God as a loving parent. Let us say the prayer Jesus taught, imaging God as a kindly father.

All Our Father, who art in heaven, hallowed be thy name, etc.

Leader Heal our imperfect human race, Holy God, of all our illnesses and mistakes. We stand in need of both your healing and your forgiveness. We are especially regretful for our ingratitude in the past, are determined to take more reverent care in the future of all your awesome gifts to us, both the persons in our life as well as our earthly habitat.

All Amen.

HOLINESS OF EARTH
God, O God of Wonders
from Psalm 8

CALL TO WORSHIP

Leader   Sing praise to God in the holy assembly.

All   For we honor God's name in all the earth.

Leader   In your presence, Holy Mystery, Creator of heaven and earth, we seek the grace of solidarity with the whole earth community, so that our children and their children can thrive on this astonishing earth-home.

All   Blest be God forever.

ANTIPHONAL PSALM
*(Group A—or Leader—reads **bold** lines. The others read regular lines.)*

God, O God of wonders
How holy is your name throughout the earth
     God of stars and thunders
     How holy is your name throughout the earth

Behold, our infant children sing your *Kyrie*
And make your glory ring above the sky
The beauty of the daffodils is eloquent
And crickets chant your praises when they cry
     God, O God of wonders
     How holy is your name throughout the earth
     God of stars and thunders
     How holy is your name throughout the earth

You tower over evil in your majesty
We look in awe at your night sky above
The stars and moon, the magic of your fingertips
The Universe, a miracle of love
     God, O God of wonders
     How holy is your name throughout the earth
     God of stars and thunders
     How holy is your name throughout the earth

**You juggle massive stars and giant galaxies
So, how concerned with humans can you be
But you have made us partners in your universe
As if like gods and goddesses are we**

> God, O God of wonders
> How holy is your name throughout the earth
> God of stars and thunders
> How holy is your name throughout the earth

**The ox and sheep are our responsibility
And animals and beasts of every size
All birds that fly, all fish that swim, rely on us
For Earth will die unless we're strong and wise**

> God, O God of wonders
> How holy is your name throughout the earth
> God of stars and thunders
> How holy is your name throughout the earth

RELATED GOSPEL READING
Luke 1:39-55   Mary greets Elizabeth with a song of thanks.

SILENT MEDITATION

Leader   We add to Mary's canticle our own inner psalm of silence and gratitude. *(After a period of silence, the leader goes on.)*

CONCLUDING PRAYERS

Leader   Together we pray the prayer Jesus taught his disciples, approaching the Infinite God as we would a loving parent.

All   Our Father, who art in heaven, hallowed be thy name, etc.

Leader   Dear God, bless us with a little of that sense of wonder that you give to your saints. With awe for all your creation, we can live more gratefully in your presence, and always be worthy of our responsibilities and vocation, confident that you have forgiven us for our past failings and have promised us your never-failing love.

All   Amen.

FAITH
Your Eyes Have Searched My Soul
from Psalm 139

CALL TO WORSHIP
Leader   Grace and peace be yours from God and from the Lord Jesus.

All   Blest be God forever.

Leader   Divine Spirit, draw us into your light, illuminate our minds with a knowledge of you, and give us energy to search for you where you can be found: first in the pursuit of justice, and then in the light of prayer.

All   May the Divine Presence fill our minds and our hearts.

ANTIPHONAL PSALM
*(Group A—or Leader—reads **bold** lines. The others read regular lines.)*

O God, your eyes have searched my soul
You've known me utterly
You know when I sit down and when I rise
   You know the roads I walk along, you know where I lie down
   You know my fond delusions and disguise

    Before my thought becomes a word
    You know what I will say
    You know my past, my present, and my plans
       You lay a kind and loving hand of comfort on my head
       You hold me, with the cosmos, in your hands

Where might I go to hide from you
My Lover and my God?
If I ascend the heavens, you are there
   You'd find me in the house of death
   You'd find me in the dawn
   Or far at sea—you'd find me anywhere

If I should say, "I'll hide myself
  in darkness and in night"
The darkest dark is bright as day to you
  To you I turn my human face
    and know that you are there
      Your Presence almost too good to be true

RELATED GOSPEL READING
John 17:24-26 Jesus prays at the Last Supper.

SILENT MEDITATION

Leader   Now, feeling completely known by God, we give silent thanks. *(After a period of silence, the leader goes on.)*

CONCLUDING PRAYERS

Leader   "Lord, teach us to pray," asked the disciples. Let us now recite the prayer that the Lord Jesus taught them, imagining the infinite God hearing us with the compassion of a kindly father.

All   Our Father, who art in heaven, hallowed be thy name, etc.

Leader   Dear Parenting Spirit, unthreatening and liberating, we thank you for all you have done for us, especially for the constant joy of knowing you are present, with us, in us and around us. Teach us to be, like you, present to and generous to those who need us and depend on us.

All   Blest be God forever.

PEACE OF MIND
I Am Filled With Anxiety
Psalm in Silence

CALL TO WORSHIP

Leader   The grace and peace of the Lord Jesus Christ be with you.

All   And also with you.

Leader   Let us pray this psalm in the silence of our hearts. *(If all do not have a copy, Leader says: "We open our hearts to this meditation before the face of God present among us and within us." Then the Leader reads the meditation.)*

Mysterious Spirit of Love and Life
When I look at the long list of things I might do today
    I am filled with anxiety
      —until I realize that there is plenty of time
      for those things which you want me to do
It is from you that I receive both the task *and* the time to do the task:
    they are perfectly matched.
Other thoughts I will have to set aside—as dreams
    perhaps for tomorrow, not for today
I submit in advance to the non-accomplishment
     of all those things you have given me no time for today
      for instance, to call my political representatives and lobby them
      to change the American economic system
        so that work is valued above ownership
        and therefore so that workers gradually get wealthy enough
          to own their own homes,
           provide security for their children and their old age
          and be able to afford excellent health care
I haven't time today to accomplish that

And I have no time to get downtown to collect the homeless
     and care for their needs
     to find all the hurting children
     and establish them in loving homes
I do not have time today to read the books
     that will make me knowledgeable enough
       about abusive customs and practices
     so that my city and my nation and my world

> can become fully human
I haven't the time it might take me
> to halt the pollution of our atmosphere
> and our systematic destruction of Mother Earth
I am unable today to invent a better social system
> so that women and men can find proper partners for each other
> so that education for the young and old
>> can become truly enlightened
> so that the elderly are all tenderly cared for
> and the hurting healed to the best of our ability
I haven't time today to bring into being
> all the daycare centers we need
> all the job training that isn't being provided to those seeking it
>> and all the freedom from coercion and manipulation
>>> that every political system should enjoy
I just don't have the time

But I do give thanks for your generous gift
> of plenty of time
> to do everything you ask of me. Amen.

RELATED GOSPEL READING
John 2:7-11   Jesus changes plain water into wine.

SILENT MEDITATION

Leader   In gratitude and inner surrender, let us rejoice over the talents God has given us. *(After a period of silence, the leader goes on.)*

CONCLUDING PRAYERS

Leader   "Lord, teach us to pray," we ask along with the disciples. Let us now recite the prayer that the Lord Jesus taught the disciples, imagining the infinite God as a father.

All   Our Father, who art in heaven, hallowed be thy name, etc.

Leader   We trust in you, Holy God of time and eternity. Bless us with the grace of wisdom, understanding of our worldly tasks, and patience in carrying them out. For we know you look upon us not only with high hopes and encouragement, but also with love and sympathy. Amen.

All   Blest be God forever.

Index

Psalms for Liturgical Seasons

Psalms for Advent	**Page** 12	Psalms for Lent	**Page** 28
	14		30
	16		33
			34
Psalms for Christmas	18		36
	20		
		Psalms for Easter	38
Psalms for Epiphany	22		40
	24		42
	26		
		Psalms for Pentecost	44
			46

Psalms for Particular Times

Psalms for Calling to Worship	**Page** 4	Psalms of Celebration	**Page** 24
	10		38
	54		48
		Psalms of Anguish	28
Psalms for Closing	6		30
	52		66
	66		
		Psalms of Joy	42
Morning Psalms	12		64
	18		74
	76		
		Psalms for Meditation	26
Evening Psalms	40		36
	60		44
	70		

Numerical List of Scriptural Psalms

Psalm			Page	
	8	God, O God of Wonders		74
	16	You Are My Heart's Home		6
	17	Come Hear My Prayer		64
	22	Why Have You Forsaken Me?		28
	25	In You I Trust		12
	27	My Light and My Hope		52
	31	Into Your Hands		46
	34	Taste and See		34
	63	My Soul Longs for You		66
	72	All the Earth Is His Nation		22
	85	Come O God and Open Our Eyes		14
	95	If Today You Hear God's Voice		54
	98	Sing a New Song		18
	103	Bless Your God		60
	104	Send Forth Your Spirit		48
	118	This Is the Day		38
	119	Blest Are They		4
	130	Out of the Depths		30
	136	Give Thanks to God		40
	139	Your Eyes Have Searched My Soul		76
	145	I Will Praise Your Name		70

Alphabetical List of Poetic Psalms

Psalm		Page	
	Bless My Descendants		44
	Creation's Composer		62
	Forgive Us Our Debts		20
	God of the Unexpected		8
	Grant a Meeting of Minds		10
	How Long Must We Wait?		16
	How We Do Blunder		68
	I Am Filled With Anxiety		78
	In Memory of You		50
	Let All the World Sing		24
	Look Into the Soul		26
	Make Us Disciples		58
	Messiah, Jesus, Yeshua, Christ		36
	My Heart's Applause		42
	Praise God for Our Enemies		56
	You Are My Heart's Home		6

OTHER PRAYER SERVICE BOOKS FROM TWENTY-THIRD PUBLICATIONS

Gathering Prayers
Debra Hintz

Scripture-based prayer services to begin and end parish meetings. For all parish organizations.
ISBN: 0-89622-269-9, 88 pages, 8.5" X 11", Paper, $9.95 (order B-31)

Prayer Services for Parish Meetings
Debra Hintz

Forty prayer services based on Scripture. They can be used to open and close a variety of get-togethers.
ISBN: 0-89622-170-9, 96 pages, 8.5" X 11", Paper, $9.95 (order B-07)

Prayer Services for Religious Educators
Gwen Costello

Thirty-two prayer services for children, teens, parish ministers and families. Focuses on the liturgical year and the sacraments.
ISBN: 089622-390-6, 80 pages, 8.5" X 11", Paper, $9.95 (order W-93)

Praying With Children
Gwen Costello

Twenty-eight prayer services for a variety of occasions. Covers the seasons of the year, liturgical feasts and special occasions. For teachers, catechists and parents.
ISBN: 089622-439-2, 96 pages, 8.5" X 11", Paper, $9.95 (order C-32)

Seasonal Prayer Services for Teenagers
Greg Dues

Sixteen prayer services that help teenagers understand the themes found in the holidays of the seasons, the church year and the civic year. Each prayer service includes catechetical notes and Scripture readings.
ISBN: 0-89622-473-2, 80 pages, 8.5" X 11", Paper, $9.95 (order C-53)

The Silver Lining:
Personalized Scriptural Wake Services
J. Massyngbaerde Ford

Wake services for parish leaders, including ones for crib death, fatal auto accidents, a suicide and death after a lingering illness.
ISBN: 0-89622-331-0, 112 pages, 6" X 9", Cloth, $19.95 (order W-21)

Teen Prayer Services:
20 Themes for Reflection
Kevin Regan

These services focus on issues important to teens, such as: failure, making choices, friendship, prayer and discipline, forgiveness, sex and sexuality, giving thanks, peace.
ISBN: 0-89622-520-8, 80 pages, 8.5" X 11", Paper, $9.95 (order C-53)

Women's Prayer Services
Edited by Iben Gjerding & Katherine Kinnamon

Creative new possibilities for meaningful, contemporary prayer form for groups of women.
ISBN: 0-89622-329-9, 80 pages, 8.5" X 11", Large Print, Paper, $7.95 (order B-82)

Available at religious bookstores
or from **TWENTY-THIRD PUBLICATIONS**
P.O. Box 180 • Mystic, CT 06355 • 1-800-321-0411